KAREN LATCHANA KENNEY

THE SCIENCE OF RACE CARS

STUDYING FORCES AND MOTION

Checkerboard Library

An Imprint of Abdo Publishing
abdopublishing.com

abdopublishing.com

Published by Abdo Publishing, a division of ABDO, PO Box 398166, Minneapolis, Minnesota 55439.

Printed in the United States of America, North Mankato, Minnesota

102015
012016

THIS BOOK CONTAINS RECYCLED MATERIALS

Design: Christa Schneider
Production: Mighty Media, Inc.
Editor: Rebecca Felix

Cover Photos: Shutterstock, front cover, back cover
Interior Photos: AP Images, pp. 10, 21; iStockphoto, pp. 8, 25; Mighty Media, Inc., pp. 4–5, 7, 9, 13, 18; Shutterstock, pp. 9, 11, 12, 13, 14, 15, 16, 17, 19, 23, 26, 27, 28–29

Library of Congress Cataloging-in-Publication Data

Kenney, Karen Latchana, author.
The science of race cars : studying forces and motion / by Karen Latchana Kenney.
pages cm. -- (Science in action)
Includes index.
ISBN 978-1-62403-963-8
1. Automobiles, Racing--Juvenile literature. 2. Force and energy--Juvenile literature. 3. Dynamics--Juvenile literature. 4. Motion--Juvenile literature. I. Title.
TL236.K45 2016
629.228--dc23

2015026568

CONTENTS

INTRODUCTION

DRAFTING FOR SPEED!

Engines roar as race cars speed around the track. With a track that is miles long, there's plenty of space for the cars to race. Yet cars pair up, racing one right in front of the other. Why? Whizzing around the track in **tandem** makes both cars move faster.

The race car pairs are drafting. When drafting, billions of air molecules hit the car in front, creating high pressure there. The air pushes on the car before rolling across its top toward its rear. Low pressure is created at the back of the car, which slows the car down.

When two cars draft, the air flow is directed over both cars as if they were one car. The first car breaks through high pressure air but is not slowed down by low pressure at its rear. The second deals with low pressure at the back but does not have to break through high pressure air at its front. So, both cars get a boost of speed.

FORCES AND MOTION

CHAPTER 1

Motion is energy in the form of movement. It's easy to see the motion of race cars. They whip around the track at super fast speeds. But for a race to begin, the cars need to get going.

Force is needed to set objects in motion. Engines provide this force in race cars. Force can also increase an object's speed. As the object moves, it pushes back equally against the force. On a race track, the force of air pushes on the cars, affecting their motion and speed. The force of the car's weight affects how well its tires grip the asphalt.

Studying forces and motion helps car designers build safer race cars. And mastering the effects of different forces helps drivers reach top speeds.

MEASURE IT

MEASURING MOTION

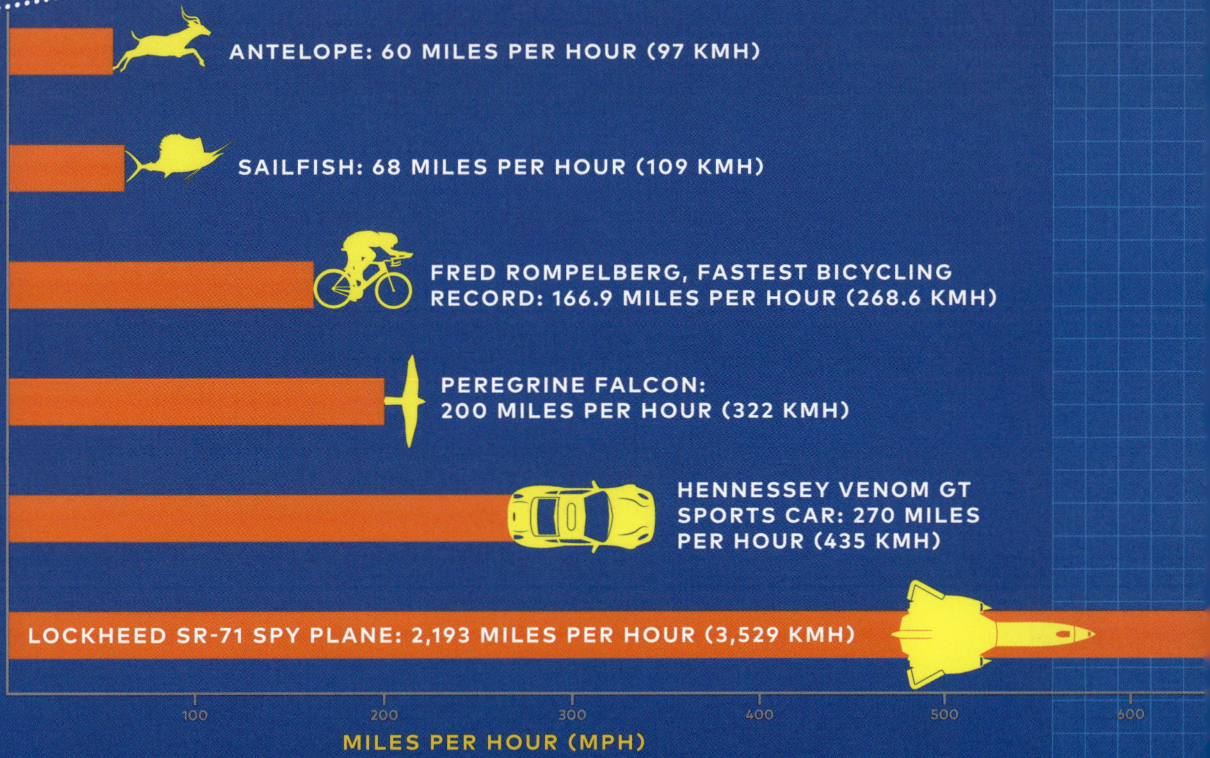

Racing is all about speed. An object's speed is found by dividing the distance it covered by the time it took to travel. The speed of a race car is measured in miles or kilometers per hour. This graph shows some of the top speeds found in our world.

READY, SET, RACE!

CHAPTER 2

Cars line up and drivers start their engines. It's time to put force to work to set the cars in motion! This force comes from a series of explosions inside the engine. The explosions occur when a chemical reaction with the right combination of fire, oxygen, and fuel is created.

This reaction occurs within the engine's cylinders. Rounded metal pieces called pistons move up and down inside cylinders in four stages. The first stage is the

Race car drivers line up in a grid at starting lines. Their position is often based on previous wins.

intake. The piston moves from the top to the bottom of the cylinder. A **valve** at the top of the cylinder opens to suck in a mixture of gas and air. The valve closes and the piston moves up, compressing the mixture. Next, a spark **ignites** the mixture, causing it to explode and create hot gases. The force of this explosion pushes the piston down.

In the last stage, the piston moves up again, pushing the gases. A valve opens to release the gases as exhaust. The motion from this cycle moves the car's **crankshaft**, and then **drivetrain**, creating the force that moves the car's wheels. The cars are ready to race!

PISTON POWER

The **combustion** cycle of an engine

1. INTAKE
2. COMPRESSION
3. SPARK
4. EXHAUST

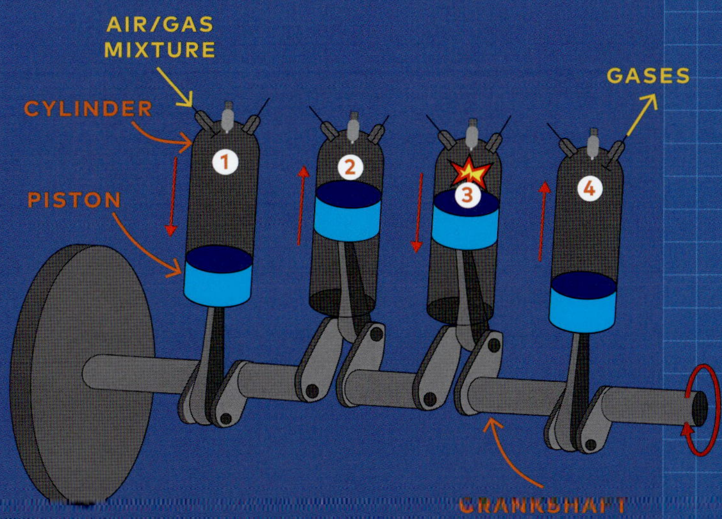

ENGINE FRICTION

Race car engines work incredibly hard during races. Engine parts move constantly in a repeating motion. These metal parts rub against each other, creating fiction. This force can cause a lot of damage inside an engine.

Friction occurs when two objects try to slide against each other. The rubbing of one object against the other other slows or stops this sliding action. As it does so, heat energy is released.

A steaming race car overheats at a race in Spain, ruining the car's engine.

Oil is important for reducing friction in both race car and everyday car engines.

Friction wears down engine parts. Too much friction can even cause engine failure. The heat from the friction can **meld** metal parts together, making movement impossible.

Engine oil is the key to fighting friction. This slippery liquid clings to metal. It thinly coats the metal parts, easing friction and helping them slide easily against each other. This reduces heat in the engine. It also keeps engine parts moving as fast as possible so the race car can move as fast as possible too!

SPEEDING UP

CHAPTER 3

Engines roar at the starting line. Drivers hit their gas pedals, and the race is on! Race car engines quickly change fuel energy from their engines to motion energy at their wheels.

Formula 1 cars can reach speeds up to 240 miles per hour (386 kmh). What does that speed tell us? If the race lasted one hour, the car would travel a distance

Speeding race cars create a motion blur of colors as they whip around a track.

equal 240 miles (386 km). But the car would have to maintain that speed for the entire time. Race car drivers generally slow down when taking corners. On straight stretches of track, they **accelerate**.

Acceleration is the result of unbalanced forces on the car. The car's engine creates a forward force. This force is greater than the force of the air pushing back on the car. Race cars accelerate very quickly.

A race car's mass is also important to its acceleration. Using the same forward force, a lighter car will travel farther than a heavier one.

MASS AND ACCELERATION

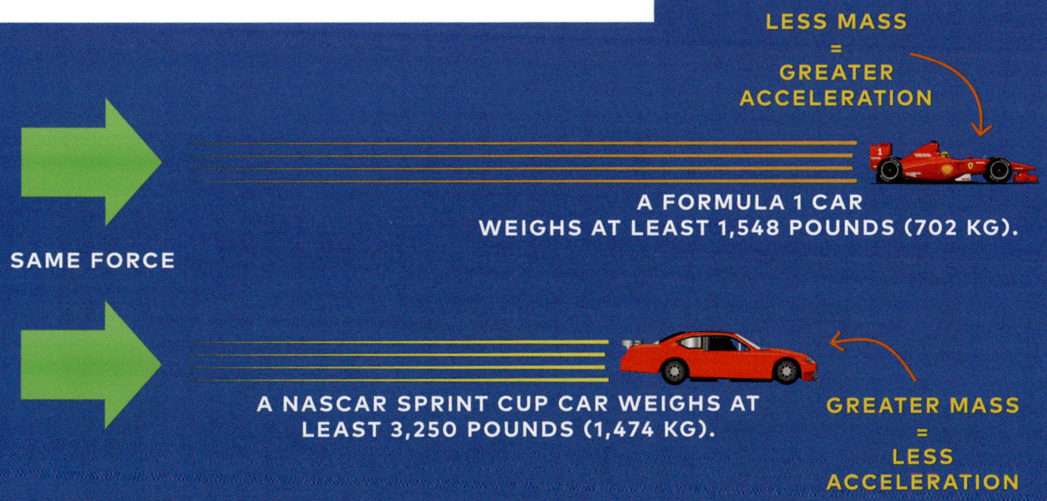

GOOD GRIP

How well a race car's tires grip the asphalt is extremely important. This grip keeps the car on the track. Friction is the enemy of the car's engine. But for good tire grip, friction is essential.

Spinning tires rapidly rub against the track during a race, creating friction. This causes the car's wheels to stick to the asphalt. Friction is especially important around turns. Without good grip, tires could lift off the

Race car tires create so much friction that they quickly wear down. Drivers must stop to have new tires put on mid-race!

track. The race car could then spin out or crash as a result.

Increasing contact between the tire's rubber and the track helps create good grip. To this end, a racing tire has little to no grooves, or treads. It is very wide too. These things increase the amount of tire that comes in contact with the track.

The friction from skidding tires as race cars accelerate or brake can create smoke!

Downforce also helps improve grip. This is the force pushing down on the car. Much of this force comes from the car's weight. Downforce from weight is useful on slower corners and when starting in a race.

Downforce from air pressure is important when a car is going very fast. Air pressure creates downforce without adding extra weight. This allows drivers to get the kind of grip needed to take turns at high speeds.

WEIGHT AND GRAVITY

When a race car brakes, accelerates, or turns, its tires' grip changes. The car's weight shifts, and the downforce on each tire changes. This is called load transfer.

When braking, more weight transfers to the front wheels. Accelerating increases the load on the rear wheels. When turning, the weight can be very different on each wheel. This affects the contact points of each wheel.

Heavier downforce on certain tires can be seen in a race car's tilt after taking a corner.

Race cars are built low to the ground, creating a low center of gravity.

Sometimes wheels even lift off the track. This can lead to a car tipping over or spinning out of control. Avoiding this and keeping good grip has a lot to do with a car's center of gravity.

A car's center of gravity is an **invisible** point where the car's weight is concentrated. How high or low this point is from the ground affects how much weight shifts during a car's load transfer.

More weight transfers on cars with higher centers of gravity. That's why race car designers create cars with low centers of gravity. It helps keep the load transferred evenly on the tires as race cars make fast turns. Each tire's contact points with the track stay as even as possible. This allows drivers to keep up high speeds and resist tipping on the track.

BANKED TURNS

Turning is tricky on race car tracks. When a race car moves around a curve, its **inertia** causes it to push away from the center of the track.

Objects in motion resist changing direction. Before a corner, a race car is traveling a straight road. On a curve, the road moves inward, toward the center of the track. The car resists, pushing to keep its straight direction. To **counteract** this and make the turn, **centripetal force** is needed.

A car traveling straight on a race track will continue in that direction *(turquoise)*, instead of the direction of the curve *(green)*. Centripetal force *(yellow)* draws the car toward the center of the curve *(red)*.

Different tracks bank at different angles. Some are very steep.

Friction between the tires and the track provides some of this force. The way race tracks are built provides the rest. A race track's curved sections are not flat. They are banked, angling upward from the inner to the outer part of the track.

Going into a turn, the car's resistance to a change in motion causes it to push down on the track, away from the track's center. The **centripetal force** of the banked corner pushes back, toward the track's center. These combined forces allow the car to take turns at high speeds.

AIR'S POWER

Race car designers also consider the combined forces of air to increase race car speed. Remember that pairs of drivers use drafting to direct airflow while racing. But before the cars even hit the track, designers prepare them for air's power. Car designers look at a car's **aerodynamics**. They work to avoid the air's ability to slow cars down during races.

Air is filled with millions of tiny molecules that hit race cars at high speeds. If these molecules hit a vertical surface, they produce a lot of resistance. This is called drag. It can really slow a race car down.

To fight drag, designers make smooth car bodies that slope toward the rear. They use side mirrors that barely stick out from the bodies. These designs lessen the surface area of the car that hits air head-on. So, the air easily flows up and over the car.

DRAFTING CHAMP

JUNIOR JOHNSON

Junior Johnson beams from inside his car after winning a 1964 race.

Born in 1931, world-famous NASCAR driver Junior Johnson was the first person to use drafting during a race. In 1960, Johnson was practicing at Daytona International Speedway. He pulled closely behind a car and noticed it reduced the drag on his car. Less drag allowed Johnson to quickly move out of the draft to pass the car in front of him.

Johnson tried this technique in the 1960 Daytona 500. He won the race! And his drafting technique forever changed how NASCAR drivers race.

LIFT

Air flows both over and under a race car. The air hits the front of the car. It travels over the car and speeds up. The air traveling under the car slows down.

The slower air moves, the greater its pressure. This causes high pressure under the car pushing up against lower pressure above the car. This creates lift, the same force used to make airplanes fly.

Similar to an airplane wing lifting into the sky, this force can make a car's rear tires lift up off the track. This can be dangerous during a race.

To combat lift, race car designers create features to increase downforce. Take a look at a **Formula 1 car**. These light cars need a lot of downforce to travel at high speeds. To achieve this, they are made with special front and rear wings.

A Formula 1 car's front wing is low to the ground. Its rear wing sits above the car's rear tires. These wings are flatter at the top. The sides facing down are curved.

The Formula 1's front and rear wings create 60 percent of its downforce.

They are basically upside-down versions of airplane wings. The front wing directs air over the car. The rear wing pushes air down. This creates an amazing amount of downforce. The rear tires are pushed into the track, increasing the car's grip so it stays safely on the ground.

MOMENTUM PROTECTION

CHAPTER 5

A moving race car has a lot of energy. It **hurtles** down the track at super fast speeds. Crashes are always a danger. When they occur, a car's forward energy has to go somewhere. This is because energy is never lost. It simply changes from one form to another.

A race car screeches to a stop during a crash. But inside the car, the driver still has forward momentum. Seat belts keep the driver's body secure in the seat. A special device on his or her helmet attaches to the seat belt. It prevents neck and head injuries.

Race cars are designed to protect drivers during a crash. Special crumple zones at the front and rear absorb most of the car's motion energy. The car's metal deforms and breaks away. A safety cage surrounds the driver and does not break away. These designs protect drivers from the powerful transfer of motion energy.

SCIENTIST AND GREAT THINKER

SIR ISAAC NEWTON

Sir Isaac Newton was born in the 1600s. He created three Laws of Motion that describe how forces and motion work on Earth. His first law states that objects tend to travel in a straight line or remain still unless a force acts upon them.

Newton's second law describes how mass affects an object's motion. More force is needed to make objects with more mass **accelerate**. His third law states that all actions have an equal and opposite reaction.

Force is measured in newtons, named after Sir Isaac Newton.

FULL SPEED AHEAD!

CONCLUSION

It's exciting at a racetrack! Forces and motion are at work everywhere. Pistons pump as crowds hear the roar of engines firing up. Wheels grip the asphalt as cars peel away from the starting line. Friction helps keeps the spinning tires stuck to the track. **Inertia** and

The incredible effects of forces and motion are visible on race tracks for all kinds of vehicles.

Race car fans cheer and wave in the stands as cars whiz around the track in a blur of motion.

centripetal force are at work on angled corners. Air whips over and under the racing cars, nearly causing them to lift right off the track.

Special designs keep the whizzing cars on the ground as they circle the track. When a fast-moving car crashes, the car's design allows energy to transfer and absorb elsewhere so the drivers walk away from wrecks.

Race car designers understand how Earth's many forces affect race car motion. They create special safety gear and cars with intelligent features. Drivers also use forces to their advantage, applying techniques to win races at record-breaking speeds.

TOY CAR

TRACK

AN EXPERIMENT WITH FRICTION

EXPERIMENT

QUESTION

Can you increase a toy car's speed using friction and forces?

RESEARCH

You've learned that friction can affect speed and grip of a race car (page 14). What will happen when you push a toy car with equal force, but with different amounts of friction under the tire? Here's what you'll need to find out:

- 2 toy cars
- equal lengths of sandpaper and cardboard
- tape
- measuring tape

PREDICT

Make a guess about what will happen. **Predict** how each material will affect the car's speed. Write it down.

TEST

1. Tape the cardboard and sandpaper to the floor. Put the two materials side by side.

2. Put one car on the sandpaper and one on the cardboard. Push each with equal force at the same time.

3. Watch how the cars roll. Is one faster than the other? Does one travel farther before losing energy? Measure the distances each car traveled.

ASSESS

Look at your results. Which car rolled a shorter distance or traveled slower? Why? What other surfaces could you use to create friction?

GLOSSARY

accelerate – to move faster or gain speed.

aerodynamic – qualities that makes an object move easily and quickly through air.

centripetal force – the force that pulls toward the center of a circle on an object moving around that circle.

combustion – the act or instance of burning.

counteract – to act against something, making it less effective.

crankshaft – a shaft driven by a crank. In an automobile engine, the crankshaft changes the up-and-down motion of the pistons into the circular motion needed to turn the wheels.

drivetrain – the parts that connect a car's transmission with its driving axles.

Formula 1 car – a special racing car used in Formula 1 events. The driver sits in the single seat and in front of the engine.

hurtle – to move with great force and speed.

ignite – to set on fire.

inertia – an object's resistance to a change in motion.

invisible – something that cannot be seen.

meld – combine.

predict – to guess something ahead of time on the basis of observation, experience, or reasoning.

tandem – a group of two or more objects arranged one behind the other.

valve – a moveable part that controls the amount of liquid or gas that flows into something.

WEBSITES

To learn more about Science in Action, visit **booklinks.abdopublishing.com.** These links are routinely monitored and updated to provide the most current information available.

INDEX